**EVERY MINUTE
6 WAVES HIT THE SHORE.
HOW MANY WAVES WILL
REACH THE BEACH
IN 10 MINUTES?**

Word problem?

Not my problem.

2019 Catherine Fet, Leonid Erostanetsky
North Landing Books
all rights reserved

WORD PROBLEM HOUSES

Have you noticed that some math word problems are kind of similar? Compare these two problems:

Problem 1. A centipede has 50 legs on its right side, and 50 legs on its left side.
How many legs does it have in all?
Problem 2. A millipede has 500 legs on its right side, and 500 legs on its left side.
How many legs does it have in all?

Centipede... millipede...
It's the same problem, people!

Well, most math word problems fall into a few groups. We'll call them *word problem houses*. Problems of the same kind live together in the same house.

Once you know how to solve one problem from this house, you can solve any problem from this house.

MATH PROBLEMS

We'll visit each house, and first we'll solve one or two problems step-by-step together. Then I'll pick a couple problems for you to solve on your own.
To check the answers, go to the back of this book, but, hey - NO CHEATING!
First solve it, then check the answer, ok?

As we go, I'll tell you why some numbers were believed to be magical in the ancient world.

Also, you may know that some math word problems have trick questions!
I'll show you how these problems try to trick you.
We'll have a special *House of Tricks* where all the tricky word problems and puzzles live.

Let's go!

5 Steps to Solve a Word Problem

Before they invented the compass, sailors at sea used to find their way by the stars. Looking from Earth, most stars seem to travel across the sky.
However, **Polaris** — the **North Star** — stays in one place, right over the North Pole.

The sailors called it the **Star of the Seven Seas.**

Think of the North Star as the answer to your math word problem. How do you find it?

The easiest way to find the North Star is by drawing a line that connects these 2 stars of the **Big Dipper**. Follow that line, and you will find the North Star. These two stars of the Big Dipper are known as the **Pointer Stars**.

In a math word problem, the pointer stars are an equation. If you can tell the word problem story using

 **+ - ÷ or X**,

you've got your pointer that will take you straight to the answer.

For example, here is a word problem:

There are 7 jewels in a treasure chest guarded by a dragon.
But the treasure map says there should be 12 jewels there.
How many jewels did the dragon steal
for its Halloween costume?

How to tell this story using
plus or minus?
This is usually the hardest part
in solving word problems.

Word problems often tell their stories out of order.
And this can confuse you. If I told the jewels word
problem story in order, it would go like this:

There were 12 jewels in a treasure chest.
A dragon stole some jewels.
Now we have only 7 jewels left.
How many jewels did the dragon steal?

The stars of the Big Dipper don't stand still.
As seen from the Earth, the Big Dipper rotates around
the North Star counterclockwise. Its stars are always
in a new place, but the Pointer Stars keep pointing
at the North Star, no matter where they are.

Math word problems can be all over the place with their
stories and numbers, but there is always a pointer in them.
It's the relationship between what you know,
and what you don't know in a word problem.

So here are our 5 steps to solving a word problem.

Step 1
Make a list of what we know and what we don't know.

We know:
there are 7 jewels in the treasure chest
long ago there were 12 jewels in the treasure chest
We don't know:
how many jewels were taken by the dragon.

Step 2
Try to put this list in the order in which events
in the story actually happened.

What was in the beginning? The 12 jewels in the chest.
What changed? The dragon took some jewels,
but we don't know how many.
What is the result? 7 jewels left.

Step 3
Try to retell this story with numbers only.

We had a big number, 12.
It became smaller.
The result is 7.

Step 4
Tell this story using $+$ $-$ $\div$ or $\times$
This will turn your story into an equation.

We can tell this story
using subtraction,
because the dragon
subtracted (stole!)
some jewels
from the treasure chest.
$12 - ? = 7$
This is our equation,
the story told in the language of math.

Step 5
Solve the equation!

Now that we have our pointer, it's easy!
We need to find the difference between 12 and 7.

To find the difference between any two numbers, just take the bigger number and subtract the smaller number.

12 - 7 = 5 jewels stolen!

That's why, if I had a treasure chest, I wouldn't ask a dragon to guard it!

"But I needed them for my costume!"

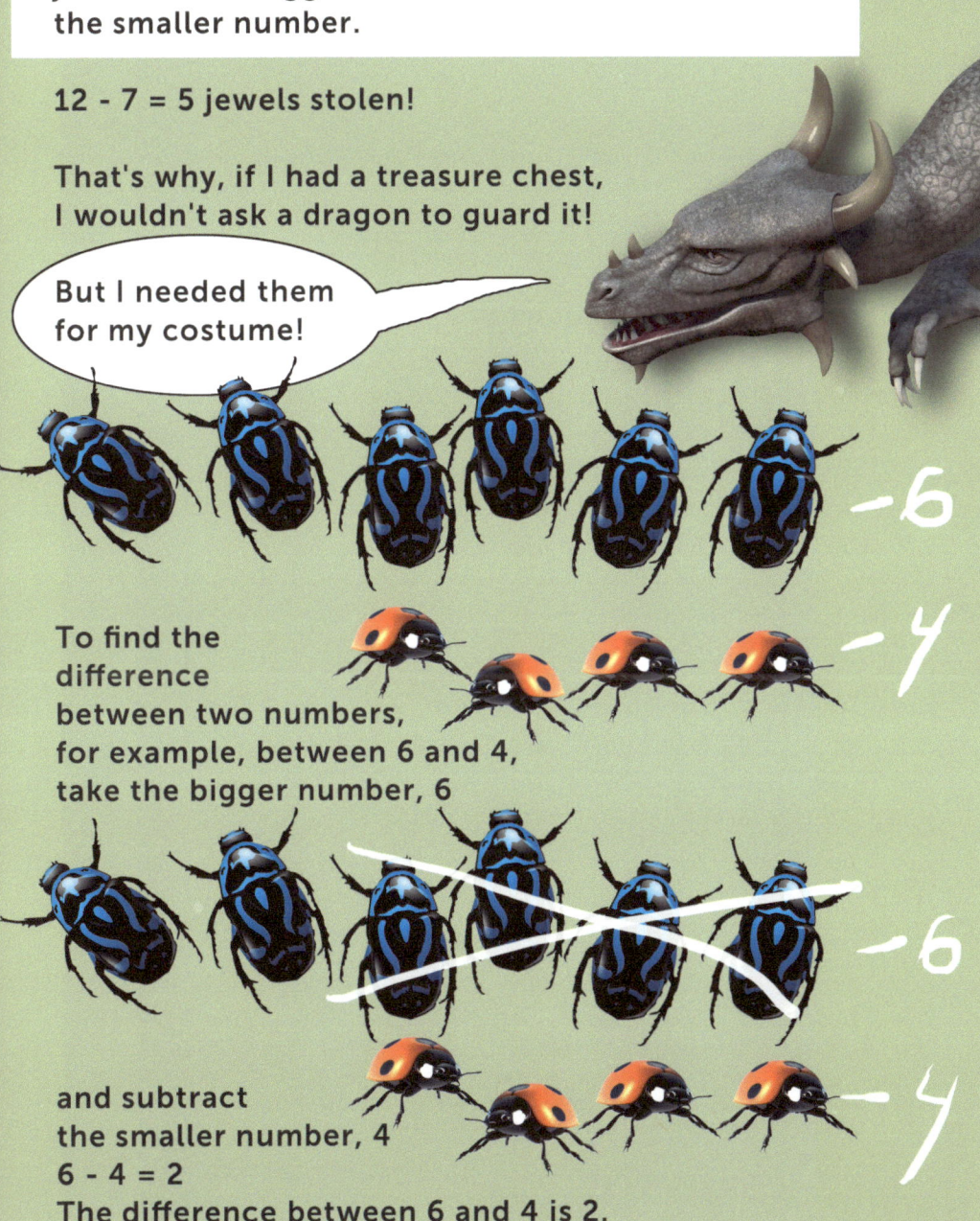

To find the difference between two numbers, for example, between 6 and 4, take the bigger number, 6

and subtract the smaller number, 4
6 - 4 = 2
The difference between 6 and 4 is 2.

All our Addition and Subtraction word problem houses
will start with the letters AS (A = addition, S = subtraction).

HOUSE AS1
THE WHOLE IS UNKNOWN

A lot of math word problems tell stories where
two or more parts make a whole.
part + part = whole
blue + yellow = green
horse + horn = unicorn
fluffy tail + long ears + the rest of it = bunny

Often, you know both parts,
and you need to find the whole:
part + part = ?
blue + yellow = ?
horse + horn = ?

If you see words like t**otal, in all, combined, together,**
or **sum**, that means they are asking you to find the whole.
Just add the two parts together and you are done!

For example:

An early bird ate 33 worms in the morning.
And it also ate 5 worms in the afternoon.
How many worms did it eat in all?

Word problems in this house are real easy,
so we'll go straight to our equation:
33 + 5 = 38
Goodness, that's a lot of worms...
That was one hungry bird!

OK, now it's your turn to solve a problem or two,
but since all the word problems in this house are so simple,
I'll add a special twist to them...

1. One of the largest buildings in Ancient Rome was the Temple of Jupiter. Ancient Romans believed that Jupiter was the god of thunder and lightning, and the king of all gods.

Unfortunately, there was a huge fire at the temple, and then an earthquake, and the building was destroyed. Ever since, people wondered what happened to the treasures of the temple. Maybe they were still hidden somewhere under the temple floor!

Two thousand years later, archaeologists were studying the ruins of the temple. Suddenly, they noticed an ancient Roman treasure map carved on a flat piece of stone! It was a piece of the marble floor from the Temple of Jupiter!
Here is the map. See the arrows and the signs?
These signs are numbers! Roman numbers were different from the numbers we use today.

Ancient Romans spoke Latin, so the archaeologists looked up the Roman numbers (also called **Roman Numerals**) in a Latin-English dictionary. Here is a page from that dictionary.

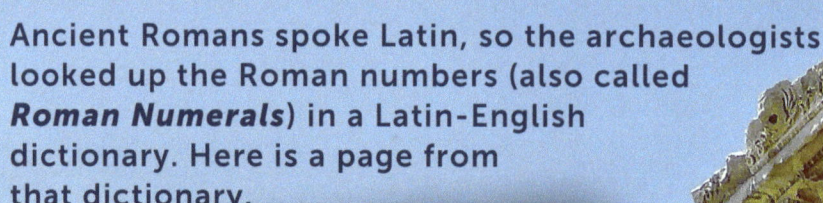

We need to translate these numbers:
Forward IV steps + XII steps
To the right IX steps + VII steps

How many steps forward and how many steps to the right should the archaeologists take to find the treasure?

By the way, the English alphabet and the alphabets of other European languages are based on the Roman Latin alphabet, which has 26 letters.

If I knew Roman numerals, that treasure would be mine!

I'll lay my hands on that dictionary! ...Oops.. I don't have any hands!!!

2. One day, in ancient Egypt, an artist was painting pictures on the walls inside a pyramid.
He was so busy that he didn't notice when the work day ended and everyone left. All of a sudden, he was alone deep inside the pyramid.
The artist was scared. He knew that at the bottom of the pyramid there was a snake pit with hundreds of snakes that came out at night to hunt. He started looking for a way out, and found this map. The map said there was a secret door!

He had to take a few steps to the right, then walk a few steps up the stairs to find the secret door.

Ancient Egyptian numbers looked very different from the numbers we use now.

Take a look at this papyrus scroll. It translates ancient Egyptian numerals into ancient Roman numerals.

| | | ||| |||| |||||
I II III IV V

∩∩   ͡ϱ   ⋀
X   C   M

Let's help the artist find his way out! How many steps forward should he take, and how many steps up should he climb, to find the secret door?

∩∩ + ∩ ||||| = ?

||| + ∩ |||| = ?

The numbers we use today are often called **Arabic Numerals.**
They were developed in India 1500 years ago, and became so popular with Arab mathematicians in Baghdad, that people started calling them Arabic Numerals. Baghdad is an Arab city. Today it's the capital of Iraq.

HOUSE AS2
TWO-STEP ADDITION WORD PROBLEMS

Some problems may have more than 2 parts and need 2 steps to solve.
We call them 2-step problems.
part + part + part = whole
blue + yellow + an easter egg = a green easter egg

Let's solve a couple word problems like these.

A caterpillar ate 5 leaves of the cabbage plant in the morning. A grasshopper ate 10 leaves of the same plant in the afternoon. By the time a bunny showed up in the vegetable garden at night, there were only 3 leaves left, and the bunny ate them all.
The farmer was real mad the next morning! How many leaves did the cabbage plant have in all before it was eaten?

Let's count all the leaves those crazy creatures ate:
Step 1: Caterpillar and grasshopper ate 5 + 10 = 15 leaves
Step 2: Caterpillar and grasshopper, plus a bunny, all together ate 15 + 3 = 18 leaves

I can totally see why the farmer was so angry. I would cry if this happened in my vegetable garden!

Not even one leaf left?

My vacation is 2 weeks and 5 days long.
How many days is it in all?
Careful! You have to go from weeks to days!
Step 1: There are 7 days in each week, so 2 weeks is
7 days + 7 days = 14 days
Step 2: My vacation is 14 days + 5 days = 19 days.
A good long vacation!
After doing all this math, I need a vacation!

Your turn to solve a problem!

1. On Halloween, a vampire decided to scare kids who were trick-or-treating. He climbed up a tree and pretended he was a zombie squirrel.
When the kids were passing under the tree, the vampire howled, ground his teeth, and threw nuts at the kids. One of the kids was so scared he dropped 3 candy bars he just got trick-or-treating. One girl started screaming and lost a lollipop out of her mouth, and yet another kid dropped 10 chocolates from his pockets as he ran away.
How many pieces of candy ended up on the ground?

2. In the ancient world people believed that 3
was a magical number.
They said 3 was the number of time:
Past • Present • Future | Beginning • Middle • End
Also 3 is the first number that forms
a geometrical figure — the triangle!
In English we say *Third time's the charm*.
There are 3 primary colors: Red, Yellow, and Blue.
In fairy tales characters often come in threes, like
The Three Little Pigs.
Many games have 3 parts, like *Rock, Paper, Scissors*.

In Ancient Greece people told stories about
all sorts of monsters. Some of them had 3 heads!
For example, they said that
Cerberus, the dog who guarded **Hades,**
the underground world of the dead, had 3 heads.
Chimera, a fire-breathing monster, had 3 heads -
the heads of a lion, a goat, and a snake!
Hydra, a poison-breathing monster, also had 3 heads.
Believe it or not, in Greek myths, these 3 monsters
were all siblings (brothers or sisters).
Their mother was Echidna, who was
half a beautiful woman, and half a snake!

*So when Cerberus, Chimera and Hydra were puppies,
and ran around the playground, how many heads
did the three of them have in all?*

3. Most starfishes have 5 arms, but the *Reef Starfish* that lives in the ocean around *New Zealand* has 11 arms. See the picture below! It's a hungry predator, eating mostly mussels. It breaks the mussel shell with its 11 arms, then it spits out its own stomach, stuffs the mussel into it, and swallows the stomach back!! Can you believe it? So gross!

So if we have 2 Reef Starfishes and 1 regular 5-arm starfish hunting together, how many arms do they have in all?

Wow, aren't we lucky we are not mussels...

If I had 11 arms, how many mussels could I eat a day?

Niam...niam... Do your math!

HOUSE OF TRICKS 1
IT DOESN'T CHANGE!

This is our first trick question word problem house.

Very often the trick question is about something that doesn't change, but the word problem tricks you into thinking that it might change.

For example:

A girl is 3 years older than her brother.
How much older than her brother will she be in 7 years?

Do you see the trick?
In 7 years she will still be 3 years older than her brother!
Both kids will be 7 years older,
but the difference between their ages will still be 3 years!
You see? That's how they try to trick you!

OK, how about this problem:

It takes me 4 minutes to cook an egg.
How many minutes will it take me to cook 3 eggs?

HOUSE AS3
ONE OF THE PARTS IS UNKNOWN.

Sometimes, you know the whole and one of the parts,
but the other part is unknown.
The unknown part can be the first part -
something that is there at the start of the problem:
? + blue = green
? + horn = unicorn
or it can be the second part, the part that brings the change:
yellow + ? = green
horse + ? = unicorn

If I show you 2 fingers, and I keep the other fingers on my hand hidden. How many fingers are hidden?

Make a list of what you know:
You see 2 fingers.
You also know that my hand has 5 fingers in all.
What you don't know is
how many fingers are hidden.

Now let's tell this story using only numbers.
We have the number 2
We also have a secret number
Together they make 5.

We'll use + to tell this story in an equation,
because we have 2 parts that make a whole.
2 + ? = 5

If one of the parts is unknown, take the whole,
which is the biggest number in your problem,
and subtract from it the part you know.
whole − known part = unknown part

5 - 2 = 3

Do I have any unknown parts?

This works no matter which part is missing,
the first or the second.

The unknown is the beginning of the problem.
? + horn = unicorn
Let's take the whole, the unicorn,
and erase (or subtract) its horn.
unicorn – horn =
What's left?
A horse!

The unknown is the change in your problem:
horse + ? = unicorn
What do you add to a horse to make it a unicorn?
Take the whole and subtract the part you know:
unicorn – horse = ? What's left? A horn!
That's what you need to add
to make it a unicorn!

Let's solve a couple problems
like this together.

**An alien spaceship collected
some red magical crystals on Mars.
Then it flew to Venus and collected
7 purple magical crystals.
Now the aliens have 27 magical crystals.
How many crystals are the red ones from Mars?**

As you solve these problems, draw a picture -
it's a great way to find your answer real quick.

What we know:
There are 7 purple crystals
The total number of crystals is 27
What we don't know:
The number of red crystals.

Let's put the events in order:
What was there at the start? A secret number of red crystals.
What changed? Aliens found 7 more crystals.
What is the result? 27 crystals.

Now let's retell this story using only numbers:
There was a secret number
We added 7 to that number
The total is 27.

The total, or the whole, is always
the biggest number in addition problems.

So here is our equation: ? + 7 = 27

To find the missing part,
we take the whole, 27,
and subtract from it the part we know, 7
27 - 7 = 20
So the aliens have 20 red crystals from Mars.

A centipede, who has a 100 legs, hides from the rain under a leaf. Then a ladybug crawls under the leaf too. The total number of legs under the leaf is now 106. How many legs does the ladybug have?

What we know:
a centipede has 100 legs
a centipede and a ladybug together have 106 legs
What we don't know:
the number of legs on a ladybug!

Let's put the events in this story in order,
and retell it using only numbers:
What was there at the start? Number 100
What changed? A secret number was added to it
What is the result? 106

Our equation is: 100 + ? = 106

To solve this problem, first we take the whole,
the biggest number in the problem, 106, and
subtract from it the part we know, 100.
106 - 100 = 6 There you go! The ladybug has 6 legs.

All insects have 6 legs - flies, beetles, butterflies, dragonflies!..
A centipede is not an insect, it's a *myriapod.*
Myriapod comes from Ancient Greek, and means 10000 legs.
And, by the way, spiders and scorpions are not insects at all.
They are *arachnids.* All arachnids have 8 legs!

Your turn! Solve these.

1. Explorers have entered an Egyptian pyramid looking for treasures. 5 kids saw them go in, and followed them inside. Then, suddenly, out of dark, secret tunnels, came a huge golden serpent. It was the guardian of the pyramid! It was looking forward to... The explorers and kids all screamed and ran for the exit! A total of 8 scared humans came running out of the pyramid! How many explorers went into the pyramid?

... A nice dinner!

Remember, to find the whole, look
for the biggest number in the problem...
Also, look for special words,
like 'total,' or 'in all'...

2. A Vampire's family always gives him pet bats on his birthday. The Vampire has 55 pet bats! On his 300th birthday he got 5 pet bats. How many bats did he receive before he turned 300 years old?

House AS4
Two-step word problems
where one of the parts is unknown

What if you have 3 parts
that make the whole, and
one of the parts is unknown?
blue + yellow + ? = a green Easter egg
What is the missing part?

Example.
3 explorers entered an Egyptian pyramid to look
for treasures. Some kids saw them, and, forgetting what
happened to them last time, again followed them
into the pyramid. Silly kids! It was dark and scary inside.
In one of the secret rooms the kids saw an open coffin.
In the coffin there was a mummy.
Suddenly, the mummy jumped
out of the coffin, and its eyes
were glowing red!
The kids started screaming.
3 of them were girls,
and they were screaming
louder than the boys.
All the kids and explorers,
ran for the exit. The total of
9 scared humans
ran out of the pyramid.
How many boys
came out?

What we know:
There were 3 explorers
There were 3 girl screamers
Total number of scared humans was 9.
What we don't know:
the number of boy screamers

Let's retell this story using only numbers:
We had 3. We added 3, and then added a secret number.
In the end we have 9.

Here is our equation: 3 + 3 + ? = 9
To solve it we'll subtract the known parts from the whole:
Step 1: 9 - 3 = 6
Step 2: 6 - 3 = 3 boy screamers
Scary, right?

"Don't sneak into ancient Egyptian pyramids, kids!"

Your turn!

1. Did you know that the power of engines is measured in **horsepower** or **hp**? When the first trains and cars were invented, engineers measured their power by comparing them to a horse. Invented in Germany, at the end of the 19th century, the very first cars were less than 1 horse power each! A horse was stronger than a car! But every year the engines became better and more powerful.

Take a look at these 3 cars:
This Italian car, a Fiat,
built in 1900, had
a 4 horsepower engine.

This French car, a Panhard,
built in 1902, had
a 12-horsepower engine.

But this German Mercedes car,
also built in 1902,
was much more powerful.

The horsepower of these 3 cars
together was 57 hp.

What was the horsepower
of the Mercedez?

Just for comparison,
modern race cars
can have
800-horsepower engines!

2.

There is something magical about the number 4!
There are 4 seasons,
4 cardinal directions or 4 main points on the compass
- North, South, East and West,
4 elements - Fire, Water, Air, Earth.
4 planets of our Solar system made of rock:
Mercury, Venus, Earth, and Mars.
4 planets made of ice and gas:
Jupiter, Saturn, Uranus, and Neptune.
Also most rooms have 4 corners, most animals have 4 legs.
And here is a joke about the number 4:
Why didn't the two 4's feel like dinner?
Because they already 8!

Look at this magic square.
In each row of this square, the numbers add up to 34.
For example, in the top row:
2 + 7 + 12 + 13 = 34
The numbers on the diagonals also add up to 34!
For example, 2 + 9 + 15 + 8 = 34
However, one number in the third row is missing:
5 ? 15 10
What is the missing number?

2	7	12	13
16	9	6	3
5		15	10
11	14	1	8

HOUSE OF TRICKS 2
"It Flew Away!"

Back to the trick questions!

In many trick word problems something disappears, but the problem doesn't tell you about it!

Example:
There were 5 birds sitting on a branch.
A hunter shot 1 bird.
How many birds are left sitting on the branch?

You may think it's just a subtraction problem: 5 - 1 = 4, but NO! It's a trick question!

The answer is: *Zero birds are left sitting on the branch!*
They flew away!
It makes sense: If one bird is shot,
the other birds won't remain sitting on the branch!
They'll be gone in a second!

House AS5
Subtraction where the result is unknown

whole − part = part
unicorn − horn = ?
Subtraction word problems often use words such as *gave, shared, lost, difference, less,* or *decrease*.

30 ants sat on a leaf sunbathing. A ladybug came and pushed 5 ants off the leaf to make room for itself. How many ants are left on the leaf?

Answer: Still too many!
Just kidding!
Let's retell this story using just numbers:
We had the number 30.
It became smaller by 5.
Our equation is:
30 - 5 = 25 ants.

It's your turn now. Solve these word problems...

1. *A castle had 18 underground tunnels that led to secret rooms full of treasures. But 7 tunnels were damaged in an earthquake, flooded by the ocean, and taken over by sea serpents. How many tunnels are still safe?*

2. In the ancient world the number 5
was also believed to be magical.
People thought the human body had 5 points:
2 hands, 2 feet, and a head.
We have 5 senses - taste, touch, smell, sight, and hearing.
A 5-pointed star is the ancient symbol
always used to draw stars in constellations.
Many flowers have 5 petals - wild roses, for example.
Many plant leaves have 5 points - for example, rose leaves.

*My grandmother taught me to make jam from rose petals.
So yesterday I brought home 2 roses from my garden,
a pink wild rose and a white garden rose.
I plucked their petals and put them in a bowl.
I had a total of 27 petals. Wild roses have only 5 petals,
but garden roses have many more petals than wild roses.
I was curious: How many petals did the white garden rose
have? So I removed the 5 pink petals from the bowl.
How many white petals were left in the bowl?*

WILD ROSE   GARDEN ROSE

House AS6
Two-Step Word Problems
Mixing Addition and Subtraction

Some word problems mix addition and subtraction. They are usually solved in 2 or more steps. For example:

A Princess has 50 roses in her garden. She sends 30 roses as a gift to Godmother Fairy. Then, Prince Charming brings her 15 roses from a faraway land. How many roses does the princess have now?

What was there at the start? 50 roses.
What changed?
30 roses were sent to Godmother Fairy
15 roses were brought by Prince Charming

Let's retell this story using numbers only:
We had 50.
We took away 30.
We added 15.

Our equation is:
50 - 30 + 15 = 35 roses

Anything left for me?

Another example:
*A Wizard buys a baby dragon that costs 25 gold coins.
He gives the dragon seller 2 bags of 15 coins each.
How much money does the Wizard get back in change?*

What we know:
a dragon costs 25 gold coins
a wizard paid 2 bags of 15 coins each,
that is 15 coins + 15 coins
The wizard paid more than the price of the dragon.
What we don't know:
How much the dragon seller should give back to the wizard.

In this story we have to compare 2 numbers:
the price of the dragon - 25 coins
and what the wizard paid, 15 coins + 15 coins (2 bags)
We need to find the difference
between these two numbers.
The dragon seller should give this difference
back to the wizard, because
the wizard paid more
than the price of the dragon.

> To find the difference between any two numbers, take the bigger number, and subtract the smaller number

Now let's retell this story
using only numbers:
We need to compare 2 numbers
25 and 15 + 15
So our equation is:
Step 1: 15 + 15 = 30
Step 2: 30 - 25 = 5 or
15 + 15 - 25 = 5 gold coins
The Wizard will get back 5 gold coins!
See how important it is to know some math? Next time
you are buying a dragon, make sure you get your change!

> Can I eat those extra coins? I'm hungry!

Your turn! Solve these 2-step problems.

1. Remember Hydra, the 3-headed monster from the Ancient Greek myths? The stories about this monster tell us that it lived near Lake Lerna, so they called it the Lernean Hydra. One day the great Greek hero Heracles came to Lake Lerna looking for the Lernean Hydra. But fighting Hydra was very hard. *When Heracles chopped off one of its 3 heads, 2 new heads popped up in its place! Then Heracles chopped off another one of Hydra's heads. The Hydra grew 2 more heads in its place right away! How many heads did Hydra have at that point?*

2. Many people around the ancient world believed that the number 6 was magical. Why? If you add the first three numbers, the sum is 6! 1 + 2 + 3 = 6 Snowflakes have 6 arms. Each tiny cell of a honeycomb has 6 sides! Fortune tellers who use playing cards believe that sixes are the luckiest cards in the card deck.

Joke about number 6:
Why is the number six so scared? Because seven eight nine! Haha! And here is our magical number 6 word problem!

One day a witch was making some magic, using the magical number 6. She first mixed water with gold powder and filled 12 cups. Then she dipped a magic silver spoon into 6 of those cups, and poured them out under a scary yew tree behind her house. As she poured them out, she cast a spell. She set aside the rest of the cups for a magic potion. She poured them into her cauldron, and added 6 more cups of water mixed with rose petals. How many cups of water were used to make the magic potion?

3. In 1588 Spanish King Phillip sent 130 ships to England. The ships carried a huge army. The ships and the army are known as *the Spanish Armada*.
King Phillip hated Queen Elizabeth of England, and wanted to defeat her. Queen Elizabeth sent her own ships to defend England. Many of the Spanish ships were galleons, very large sailing ships that couldn't move or turn fast. The English ships were smaller, faster, and had better cannons.
In the battle the English destroyed 40 Spanish ships.
The remaining Armada ships hurried back home to Spain, but the winds of the Gulf Stream, the ocean current that flows from the Gulf of Mexico all the way to England, carried the Armada ships onto rocky cliffs. 30 more ships got lost or sank. Only 3 of those 30 lost ships found their way home.
How many Spanish Armada ships came home to Spain?

This portrait of Queen Elizabeth shows the defeat of the Spanish Armada on a painting behind her.

Maybe it wasn't my best idea...

Hmmm... King Phillip doesn't look very happy on this portrait!

I told ya, Phil. Look up 'Gulf Stream' in an Encyclopedia.

HOUSE OF TRICKS 3
NO CALCULATION OR PATTERN

Some word problems and puzzles trick you into looking for a pattern in a row of letters, numbers or words. But actually, there is no pattern!

For example:
Please continue this sequence:
O, T, T, F, F, S, S, E, N....
You think it's a pattern... Maybe it's about the position of each letter in the alphabet?
Well, it's not a pattern! Guess what it is:
One, Two, Three, Four, Five, Six, Seven, Eight, Nine...

Here are a few problems from this tricky house.

1. How to make the number 666 bigger without doing any calculations?

2. Find the missing number!
See if you can solve it knowing that what you see is not a pattern!

16 | 06 | 68 | 88 | ? | 98 |

3. You have 6 matches in a row like this:
| | | | | | |
Can you add to them another eleven matches so that the result is three?

4. Here is another one!
Remember: Don't look for a pattern, look for a trick!
8138 | 4
6246 | 2
7027 | ?

HOUSE AS7
SUBTRACTION WHERE THE WHOLE OR THE START IS UNKNOWN

Sometimes we don't know the whole, or the starting number.
We know that something changes it.
And we know the result.
? - horn = horse
? - part = part

Hey, it's not the horn! It's MAGIC that makes you a unicorn.

How to solve the problems in this house?
Just add the parts and you get the whole!
horse + horn = unicorn
part + part = whole
Example:
A ladybug pushed 3 ants off a leaf to make room for its bicycle. Now it's sitting on the leaf with its bicycle and 50 angry ants.
How many ants were on the leaf in the beginning?

Let's retell this story in order:
What was there at the start? A secret number of ants on a leaf.
What changed? 3 ants got pushed off the leaf.
What is the result? 50 ants remained on the leaf.

And in numbers only:
We had a secret number.
We took away 3.
Now we have 50.
or
? - 3 = 50

To find the whole, or the starting number, let's put together all the parts we know:
3 + 50 = 53
This is the number of ants that were on the leaf before the spotted bully arrived with her bicycle!
Let's try to solve a couple problems like this.

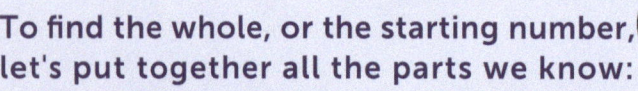
bully!

1. Our first problem in this house will use the number 7, one of the most magical numbers.
Why do so many people think 7 is magical? How about
7 days of the week, 7 continents, 7 seas
7 wonders of the world , 7 notes in a musical octave
7 colors of the rainbow, Snow White and the 7 dwarfs
Also, guess what: When you ask people to pick a number between 1 and 10, most people pick 7! Test this!

A 7-pointed shape is called a **heptagon**. A 7-pointed star can be drawn in 2 different ways without lifting your pencil from the paper!!! Try it!

If you combine these 3 figures together, you get a beautiful complex shape. Star-like shapes like this are often called **mandalas.**

And here is our word problem!

Queen Cleopatra of Egypt asked her magic teacher to turn a bunch of frogs into roses for her birthday. She gave him a bag of golden rings as payment for his magic. On the day of her birthday, the magic teacher waved his magic wand over a basket of frogs, and all except 7 of them turned into roses. Those 7 frogs didn't turn into anything. They just remained frogs in the basket saying 'ribbit, ribbit.'
Cleopatra was upset and asked the teacher to give her back 7 golden rings. After that, the magic teacher had 14 golden rings left. How many golden rings did Queen Cleopatra pay him at the start? And how much, do you think, he asked for to turn 1 frog into a rose?

Queen Cleopatra of Egypt lived in the 1st century BC. Here is her portrait, carved from marble, during one of her visits to Rome.

2. On a cloudy night, I was looking at the stars, and saw 2 constellations, the Big Dipper and the Little Dipper. I decided to count all the stars I could see. I started with the Big Dipper, and counted 7 stars. Then, suddenly, a cloud covered it, so of the remaining stars I could count only 7. How many stars are in the Big Dipper and the Little Dipper together?

Ancient Greek ship

Constantine the Great

3. Roman Emperor Constantine the Great bought some beautiful new ships from a Greek ship builder. The ships were brought to him on the coast of Italy near Rome, the capital of the Roman Empire. Soon, Constantine decided to move the capital of his empire to Byzantium, and he named his new capital after himself, Constantinople. As he moved to Constantinople, he took 15 of his new ships with him. Only 10 of these ships remained in Rome. How many ships did Constantine buy from the Greek ship builder?

HOUSE AS8
SUBTRACTION WHERE ONE OF THE PARTS IS UNKNOWN

Sometimes we have a whole, or a start number:
a unicorn
Then a part is lost, but
the word problem doesn't tell us
which part! It only tells us what is left:
a horse
We have to find the part
that was taken away.
How do we find this missing part?
Take the whole and subtract from
it the part you know.
unicorn - horse = horn!!!

Let's solve a word problem like this together.

50 happy ants sat on a leaf watching sunset. A lady bug came along and pushed some ants off the leaf to make room for a picnic. There were 30 angry ants left on the leaf. How many ants were pushed off?

Let's retell this story using only numbers:
We had the number 50.
We took away a secret number.
The result is 30.
50 - ? = 30

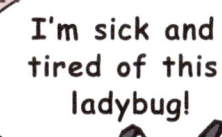

I'm sick and tired of this ladybug!

Now take the bigger number and
subtract the smaller number from it:
50 - 30 = 20
That's the number of ants pushed off the leaf.

Your turn! Let's start with another magic number - 8.

1. **What is so special about number 8?**
The mathematical symbol for infinity is an 8 on its side.
There are eight planets in our Solar System.
A spider has 8 legs, and an octopus has 8 arms!
Octopus in Greek means ***eight feet.***
A ship's wheel has 8 spokes. A cube has 8 corners.
Two squares with the same center make an 8-pointed star,
the shape that many ancient people believed was magical!
An 8-pointed figure is called ***octagon.*** Combine
an octagon with an 8-pointed star, to create
another beautiful mandala.
Take the ***4 cardinal directions***, add directions
between them, and you will have 8 directions:
North • South • East • West
North-East • North-West
South-East • South-West   *octagon*

Here is our word problem:

*A sea witch sent an octopus
to find her the best black pearls
in the deep ocean.
The octopus came back
with a black pearl in each arm.
But some of those pearls
were enchanted, and when
the witch touched them,
they melted and vanished.
Only 3 pearls remained
in her hands.
How many
black pearls
were enchanted?*

2. In the year 982, Viking Erik the Red sailed West from Iceland and discovered Greenland. In 985 he took 25 ships to Greenland. He wanted to build a town there. But a terrible storm scattered the ships around the sea, and only 14 ships came safely to Greenland. How many of Erik's ships were lost at sea?

3. *A spell is cast: Sleeping Beauty must sleep for 3 years. She has already slept for 6 months. How many more months does she have left to sleep?*
Be careful! It's a 2-step problem!
You go from years to months in this problem.
Since each year is 12 months, you must first find out how many months make 3 years - that will be your whole!

HOUSE OF TRICKS 4
TRICKY WORDS!

Some trick questions mislead you with the way they use words.
There are 7 apples on the table. Take away 3. How many do you have?

So you think: Ok, it's a subtraction problem. 7 - 3 = 4
But the answer is 3! You took 3 apples, so you have 3 apples!

We use the words *have* and *take away* in subtraction problems, and we also use these words to describe people holding or carrying things in their hands.
This is called *word play*. Word play jokes use the fact that the same word can have different meanings.

Here is an example of word play:
Time flies like an arrow. Fruit flies like a banana.
Time flies like an arrow = time goes very fast
Fruit flies like a banana = insects called 'fruit flies' enjoy eating bananas

Try these trick word problems!

1. *There are 4 cats sitting in 4 corners of a room. In front of each cat there are 3 cats, and each cat's tail is pointing at a cat. How many cats are there in the room?*

2. *If you had 4 apples and 5 oranges in one hand and 6 apples and 7 oranges in the other, what would you have?*

House AS9
Comparing, when the Difference is Unknown

How many more? or *How many fewer?*

When they ask you **how many more** or **how many fewer**, they are asking you about the difference between two numbers. Remember, to find the difference between any two numbers, all you need to do is take the bigger number and subtract the smaller number from it.

Here is a **how many more** word problem.
A ladybug has 6 legs. A spider has 8 legs. How many more legs does a spider have than a ladybug?
So take the bigger number, and subtract the smaller number from it: 8 legs - 6 legs = 2 legs!
A spider has 2 legs more than a ladybug.

And here is a **how many fewer** problem.
A ladybug has 6 legs. A spider has 8 legs. How many fewer legs does the ladybug have than the spider?

How do we find the difference here? Same way as in the **how many more** word problem. Grab the bigger number, and subtract the smaller one from it!
8 legs - 6 legs = 2 legs
The ladybug has 2 legs fewer than the spider.
Your turn! Solve these problems.

1. A princess had a vegetable garden. She fed 7 carrots from her garden to a unicorn. That night a dragon came, and ate 20 carrots. How many more carrots did the dragon eat than the unicorn?

2. Many people in the ancient world believed that the number 9 was magical, because 3 x 3 = 9, and 3 is a super-magic number! Maybe because of that we have these expressions in English:
on cloud nine • dressed to the nines • a cat has nine lives
go the whole nine yards • a stitch in time saves nine
9 out of 10 times...
Also, there are 9 square feet in a square yard. and 9 justices sit on the United States Supreme Court.

Here is our number 9 word problem:

A magic spell book says that you can cast a spell to find out your friend's secrets. You need to drop 9 white stones into a glass of rain water and wait for 9 days. After 9 days, pour that water under a green tree, and when you see your friend, they will tell you their secret.

There is another spell in the same book - a spell that helps you bury a secret. If you have a secret you don't want anyone to know, you can bury it forever, says the spellbook. Drop 3 black stones into a glass of seawater, wait for 18 days, pour that water under a dead tree, and no one will ever find out your secret. How many more days do you have to wait to bury a secret than to find out a secret?

HOUSE AS10
COMPARING, WHEN THE BIGGER NUMBER IS UNKNOWN, BUT YOU KNOW THE DIFFERENCE - 'MORE'

In some word problems that compare things, you don't know one of the things, but you know the difference between them. Sometimes the bigger thing is unknown. These problems will have words like *more, longer,* or *taller* in them.

The Tooth Fairy has 12 teeth more than my son Eric. Eric has 20 teeth. How many teeth does the Tooth Fairy have?
So, in numbers only, this word problem looks like this:
We have the number 20.
And we have another number, which is 20 + 12.
20 + 12 = 32   Our answer is 32. Your turn!

**1. A magical garden has 12 golden trees. And it also has a whole bunch of silver trees. We know that there are 7 more silver trees than golden trees.
How many silver trees are in the garden?**

My wings are bigger! Na-nana na na!

**2. A wingspan is the distance between the tips of a creature's wings. The largest bird wingspan is that of an albatross. The albatross can have a wingspan of up to 11 feet.
But in the era of dinosaurs, 68 million years ago, there were flying pterosaurs whose wingspan was 25 feet bigger than that of the albatross!
How big was the wingspan of a flying pterosaur?**

House AS11

Comparing, when the smaller number is unknown, but you know the difference - 'fewer'

Sometimes you are comparing two numbers, and you don't know the smaller number. But you know the difference between the smaller and the bigger numbers. These word problems will have words like *fewer, less,* or *shorter* in them.

Example:
A huge snake is 12 feet long. A crocodile is 7 feet shorter than the snake. How long is the crocodile?

Again, just grab the bigger number and subtract the smaller number from it.
12 - 7 = 5 feet   Your turn!

1. The **Lion's Mane jellyfish** is one of the biggest jellyfish in the world. Its tentacles can grow 120 feet long! A Sea Wasp jellyfish is the most dangerous: It's poisonous and transparent, which makes it hard to spot. But it's not as big as the Lion's Mane jellyfish. The Sea Wasp's tentacles are 110 feet shorter than the tentacles of the Lion's Mane. How long are the tentacles of the Sea Wasp?

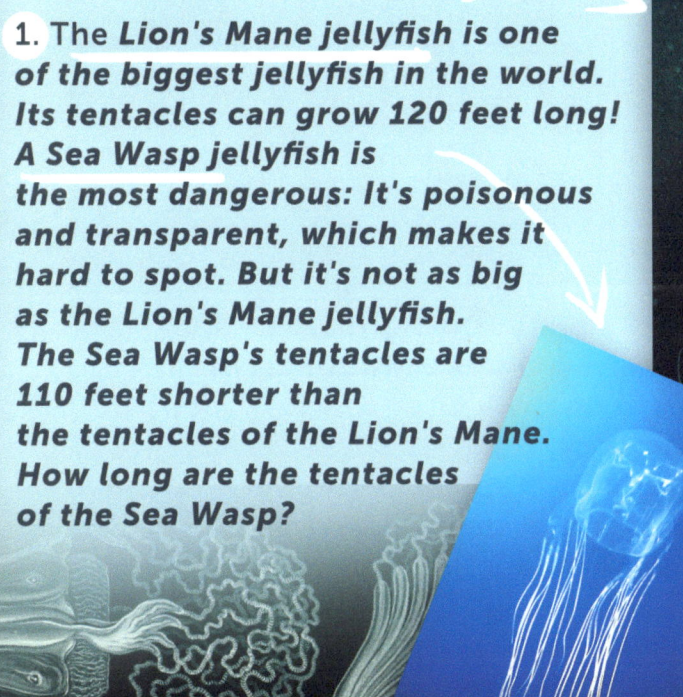

2. Did you know that a rabbit's teeth never stop growing? That's because wild rabbits eat tough, hard-to-chew plants that wear out their teeth. Most rabbits' teeth grow between 3 and 5 inches each year! Rabbits have to gnaw on something all the time to keep their teeth short.

So in this word problem, *a big white rabbit eats 15 carrots a day, but a smaller black rabbit eats 7 carrots fewer. How many carrots does the black rabbit eat every day?*

HOUSE OF TRICKS 5
ORDER PUZZLES

We know that many word problems tell a story. To find the answer you need to
• put the events in the story in the right order, and
• tell how the known and the unknown things in the story relate to each other: Is one bigger or smaller? Is one of them a whole and the other a part of it?
Once things are in order and you know the relationship between them, you build an equation, and do your calculation - add, subtract, multiply, and so on.

However, sometimes you don't need to do any calculation to solve a word problem. These word problems are called **Order Puzzles** or **Situation Puzzles.**
They tell you that to perform a task you need to do things in a special order. Your job is to figure out that order!
Here is an example.

Wolf, Goat and Cabbage

A farmer with a bucket of cabbage, a wolf, and a goat all need to cross the river. But the farmer's boat is small: It will hold only the farmer and one more item - the cabbage, the goat or the wolf. But if the farmer takes the cabbage across the river first, the wolf will stay behind with the goat, and the wolf will eat the goat! And if the farmer takes the wolf across the river first, then the goat will stay behind with the cabbage, and the goat will eat the cabbage! What to do?

Here is the solution:

Trip 1: The farmer takes the goat across the river - to the other side. The wolf and the cabbage stay behind, on this side.
Trip 2: The farmer returns to this side of the river.
Trip 3: The farmer takes the wolf across the river, but doesn't leave the goat with the wolf on the other side.
Trip 4: The farmer takes the goat back, to this side of the river and leaves it here.
Trip 5: Now the farmer carries the cabbage to the other side of the river. At this point we have the goat on this side of the river, and the wolf and the cabbage on the other side.
Trip 6: The farmer returns to this side.
Trip 7: The farmer takes the goat to the other side. Now all of them are on the other side of the river.

Here is another one. Can you figure it out?

3 soldiers need to get across the river. Two boys who are fishing in a boat nearby offer help. But the boat is small: It can hold either one grownup or two boys. How can the soldiers cross the river?

HOUSE MD-1
WE HAVE A FEW EQUAL GROUPS OF THINGS. HOW MANY THINGS IN ALL?

In our multiplication and division word problems houses M = multiplication, D = Division.

In House MD-1 word problems they always tell you there are a few bunches of things, and each bunch has the same number of things. The question is, how many things in all?
Well, all you have to do is multiply the number of bunches by the number of things in each bunch.

We have 3 bunnies.
Each bunny has 2 ears.
How many ears
do these bunnies have in all?
3 x 2 = 6 ears in all

4 princesses went for a walk.
Suddenly, a huge spider
crawled from under a castle wall.
When they saw the spider,
each princess screamed 3 times.
How many screams were heard inside the castle?

When you are solving a word problem, it's always great to draw a picture. Here we have 4 princesses. Each one screams 3 times.
4 princesses x 3 screams = 12 screams
Wow, that was a lot of screaming!

How about this one.
The Evil Queen opened a store selling poisoned apples. She arranged the apples in the store window, so they made 5 rows and 4 columns. How many poisoned apples were there in all?

Let's draw a picture.
So the rows go left to right - we have 5 of them.
And the columns go top to bottom, and we have 4 of them.

4 apples in each row. They repeat 5 times. 4 x 5 = Best poison ever!

So it's 4 x 5 = 20 apples
Someone call the police!
The Evil Queen can poison half the kingdom with these apples! Your turn!

1. Way before coins were invented, people used many different things as money. In some parts of the world they used shells. **Cowrie shells** from the Indian ocean were especially popular and used as money across Asia and Africa. In Africa they still used shell money around 100 years ago!
At that time, the shells were put together in strings, 40 or 100 cowrie shells in each string.
**50 strings of 40 shells each were equal to 1 dollar.
20 strings of 100 shells were also equal to 1 dollar.
How many shells made 1 dollar in those days in Africa?**

2. Did you know that each sunflower can make from 1000 to 2000 seeds?
*I have 8 sunflowers in my garden.
If each sunflower makes 1000 seeds,
how many seeds will I have?*

HOUSE MD-2
THE GROUP SIZE IS UNKNOWN

I need a mirror ASAP.

In this house we have word problems where things are divided into equal groups, and you know the number of things in all. You also know the number of groups. What you don't know is how many things you have in each group.

We have 3 bunnies.
*Each bunny has an unknown number of ears.
Together they have 6 ears.
How many ears does each bunny have?*
? x 3 = 6 ears
To solve this problem we need to grab all 6 ears and divide them between the 3 bunnies to see how many ears each one will get. So it's a division problem. 6 ÷ 3 = ? Hmmmm....
That won't be easy! Bunnies will kick and try to escape.
Let's try a different word problem!

*4 sharks chased 8 swimmers out of the ocean.
If each shark chased the same number of swimmers,
how many swimmers did each shark chase?*
Let's draw a picture. Here are 4 sharks chasing 8 swimmers.

In word problems like this, you grab the whole and divide it by the number of groups. You can think of it like this:
Grab the bigger number and divide it by the smaller number in your word problem.
So we take the number of swimmers and divide it by the number of sharks.
8 ÷ 4 = 2   Each shark scared 2 swimmers!

Your turn!

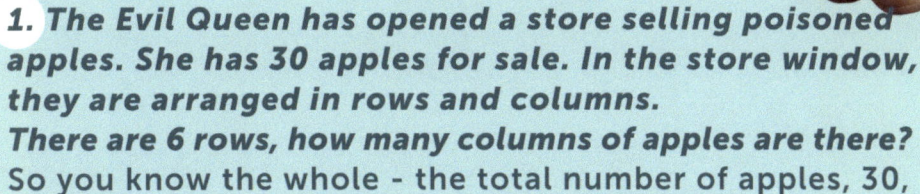

1. **The Evil Queen has opened a store selling poisoned apples. She has 30 apples for sale. In the store window, they are arranged in rows and columns.
There are 6 rows, how many columns of apples are there?**
So you know the whole - the total number of apples, 30, and the number of the groups - or rows - 6.
OK, now solve it!

2. **Clover plants usually have 3 leaves, but very rarely can you find a 4-leaf clover. People have always believed that a 4-leaf clover is a sign of great luck.**

**So, one day, a unicorn brought a bunch of clover leaves to a princess. There were 5 clovers in the bunch, and the total number of leaves was 20.
Were those 3-leaf clovers, or 4-leaf lucky clovers?**

HOUSE OF TRICKS 6
DISTRACTION!

Some word problems are not really trick problems, but they try to make you think they are more difficult to solve than they are! They distract you by giving you more information than you need to solve the problem.
Let's solve this problem:

Space aliens land on Mars, build a home there, and have 10 babies. In one month each of their babies has a baby! And the next month all those babies have a baby each! The number of aliens keeps growing. It doubles every month! Finally, in 1 year, the whole planet is covered with space aliens. How long does it take them to cover half the planet?

You may think that to solve this problem you need to multiply all those baby aliens!
But, in fact, all you need to know is this: **Every month the number of aliens doubles - which means it grows x2.** So if it takes them 12 months to cover the entire planet, one month before that their number is only half of the final number. Because once it doubles, it will cover the entire planet! So it takes them 11 months to cover half the planet. Your turn!

A witch is making a magic potion in a cauldron. She tosses dragon scales, mandragora roots, frogs' eyes and other ingredients into the potion. It starts bubbling and filling the cauldron. Every minute its quantity doubles. In 4 minutes the cauldron is full. How long did it take for the potion to fill half the cauldron?

House MD-3
The number of groups is unknown

What if you know the total number of things: 30 frogs' eyes at a witch's house. And you also know the number of things in each group: Eyes are in jars, 5 eyes per jar. But you don't know the number of groups - the jars. How many jars of frogs' eyes does the witch have?

Again, grab the whole - the biggest number in the problem, and divide it by the smaller number - things in each group. So you take the total number of frogs' eyes - 30 *(Yuck! They are slippery and disgusting!!!!)* and divide them by the other number you know - the number of eyes in each jar - 5.
30 ÷ 5 = 6 jars. Will make a nice potion! Your turn!

1. *A vampire is selling scorpions to scare kids on Halloween. He has sold 40 scorpions, 4 scorpions in each bag. How many bags of scorpions has he sold?*

Not only your friends, but also your teacher will love them!

2. In the middle of each apple, you will find 5 pockets filled with seeds. They are called **carpels**, or seed chambers. But the number of seeds in apples can vary from 5 to 13.
So if there are 5 seeds in each of my apples, and the total number of seeds in them is 40, how many apples do I have?

PUZZLE 1

You need to fill a barrel with water, so that it's exactly half-full. But you are not allowed to measure the water level. You can't use a string, a stick, or any other instrument.
How can you fill the barrel half-full?

HOUSE MD-4
COMPARING, WHEN THE SMALLER NUMBER IS UNKNOWN

Sometimes you are comparing 2 numbers. We know the bigger number. And we know that the other one is a few times smaller. We know how many times smaller it is. We need to find the smaller number.
This is a simple division problem.

Example.
A vampire eats 35 dead leaves in his dinner salad. It takes a worm a whole week to eat 5 times fewer dead leaves! How many dead leaves does the worm eat each week?

We know the bigger number - 35 dead leaves.
The smaller number we are looking for is 5 times smaller.
So take 35 dead leaves (Yuck!) and divide them by 5!
35 ÷ 5 = a worm eats 7 dead leaves each week. Your turn.

1. Did you know that the height of a horse is measured in *hands*. It's a very old tradition. A hand is 4 inches. Do you know the special words used for members of a horse family?
Stallion is a daddy horse.
Mare is a mommy horse.
Foal is a baby horse
Colt is a little boy horse
Filly is a little girl horse
So cute!
A friend of mine in Montana has two horses:
A mare, who is 16 hands tall, and her baby who is 2 times shorter than his mommy.
How tall is the colt, when measured in hands?

2. The different kinds of horses are called **breeds**. The three fastest horse breeds are the **Thoroughbred,** the **Quarter Horse,** and the **Arabian horse.** A Thoroughbred race horse can run at the speed of 50 miles per hour. A farm horse usually runs at a speed that is 2 times slower than that of a race horse. How fast is a farm horse?

House MD-5
Comparing, when the smaller number is unknown, and with trick words like 'x times more'

A vampire showed up on a playground and shouted 'Booo!' 15 little kids on the playground were scared and cried. And that was 3 times more crying kids than when the vampire shouted 'Booo!' at the 3rd grade recess. How many 3rd-graders were scared and cried?

So we know the number of the little kids who cried - 15. The number of the 3rd graders who cried is 3 times smaller. How do we find it?

Word problems like this are a bit tricky. They tell us 15 kids was **3 times more**, so they are trying to trick you into multiplying the number you know x 3, but this is a trap! Remember, if you know the bigger number, and you are looking for a smaller number, you need to make your number smaller, not bigger. You need to divide it, not multiply it! We need to make 15 three times smaller! We divide 15 by 3
15 ÷ 3 = 5 - That's the number of the 3rd graders the vampire managed to scare. Your turn!

3rd grade? They're babies!

1. A giant octopus, Kraken, sank a pirate ship. Fortunately there was an uninhabited island nearby. 15 pirates made it to the island. And that was 3 times more pirates than the number of pirates that had come to that island the day before, after their ship was sunk by a giant sea serpent. How many pirates came to the island the day before?

Uh-ohh

Remember kids, being a pirate is a dangerous profession!

2. Many people in the ancient world believed that the number 12 was magical.
12 months in a year
12 signs (or constellations) of the Zodiac
12 hours of the day and 12 hours of night
12 numbers on the face of a clock
Also, 12 is an ancient measure - *a dozen*. Eggs are sold in dozens or half-dozens. There are 12 inches in a foot. In legends about King Arthur, his round table had 12 knights. In the United States courts a jury is usually 12 people.

A fairy sprinkled fairy dust on 12 flowers. That was 3 times more than the fairy dust she sprinkled on some nearby mushrooms. How many mushrooms were sprinkled with fairy dust?

HOUSE MD-6
COMPARING, WHEN THE LARGER NUMBER IS UNKNOWN

In this house of word problems we compare 2 numbers. One is a few times bigger than the other.

Example.
A magic wand costs 7 gold coins. A spell book costs 3 times as much. How much does the spell book cost?

If a spell book costs 3 times as much as a magic wand, it costs the same as 3 magic wands!
7 coins x 3 = 21 gold coins

So to solve this problem, we took the number we know and multiplied it by 3 because we are told the other number must be 3 times bigger.

Another example. *A pig splashed dirt on 4 geese. They used to be white but now they are brown. However, there are still a lot of white geese on the lake. Actually, there are 6 times more white geese on the lake, than brown ones. How many geese are still white?*

So, again, we start with the number we know: 4 dirty geese. Now we look for the number that tells us how many times bigger the other number must be.
We know that the number of clean geese is 6 times bigger than the number of dirty geese.
So we multiply these two numbers.
4 x 6 = 24 clean white geese. This is our answer. Your turn!

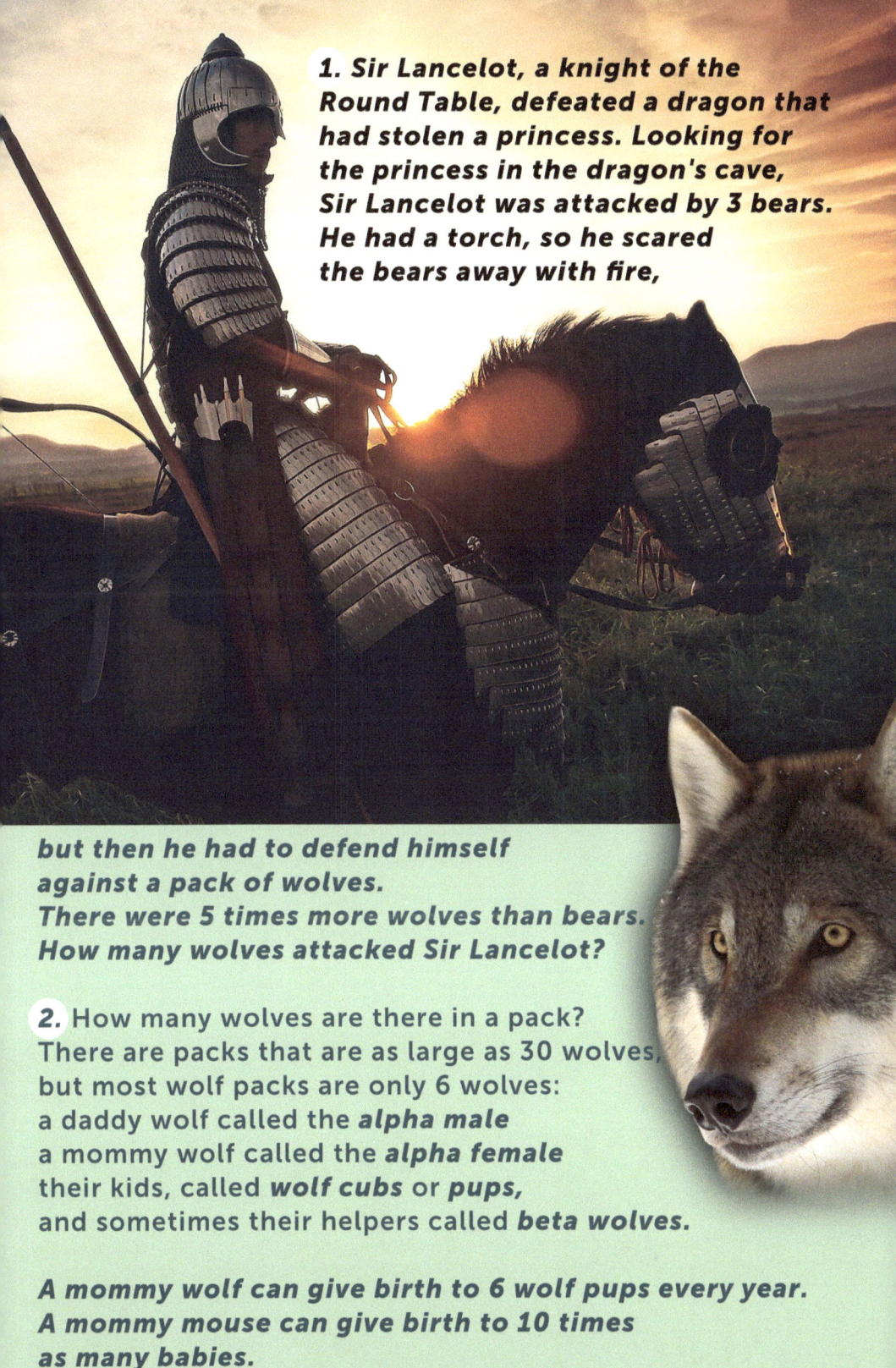

1. Sir Lancelot, a knight of the Round Table, defeated a dragon that had stolen a princess. Looking for the princess in the dragon's cave, Sir Lancelot was attacked by 3 bears. He had a torch, so he scared the bears away with fire, but then he had to defend himself against a pack of wolves.
There were 5 times more wolves than bears.
How many wolves attacked Sir Lancelot?

2. How many wolves are there in a pack?
There are packs that are as large as 30 wolves, but most wolf packs are only 6 wolves:
a daddy wolf called the *alpha male*
a mommy wolf called the *alpha female*
their kids, called *wolf cubs* or *pups,*
and sometimes their helpers called *beta wolves.*

A mommy wolf can give birth to 6 wolf pups every year.
A mommy mouse can give birth to 10 times as many babies.
How many babies can a mommy mouse have every year?

Puzzle 2

On the playground, kids were riding bicycles and tricycles.
They had 8 bicycles and tricycles,
with a total of 21 wheels.
How many bicycles and how many
tricycles were on the playground?

House MD-7
comparing, when the larger number is unknown, with trick words like 'less' or 'fewer'

In some word problems you know
the smaller number, and you are looking
for a bigger number. But all they tell you
about the bigger number is that
the smaller number is a few times smaller
than the bigger number. Again, this is tricky!

Take a look at this example.
*A witch cast 7 spells this week, and
that's 3 times fewer than the spells
cast this week by Fairy Godmother!
How many spells has
Fairy Godmother cast this week?*

So you know that the witch cast
7 spells. Then you see the words
3 times fewer, and you may be
tricked into looking for a smaller number.
Don't be tricked!
You are looking for a bigger number!
So if the smaller number is 7,
and it's 3 times fewer than
the bigger number,
you need to grow it 3 times over
to find the bigger number.
7 spells x 3 = 21 spells   Your turn!

1. Lake Baikal in Siberia, Russia is the deepest lake in the world. It is 5 thousand feet deep, and in some places even deeper. But it's 7 times less deep than the Mariana Trench in the Pacific Ocean, which is the deepest ocean area in the world. How many thousand feet deep is the Mariana Trench?

2. In the times of the dinosaurs, the famous dinosaur predator Tyrannosaurus Rex was 40 feet long from the tip of its nose to the end of its tail. And it was 2 times shorter than the Brachiosaurus who ate leaves from the tops of trees! How long was the Brachiosaurus?

Puzzle 3

Here is a scale. You have 3 types of weights - balls, square boxes, and rectangular boxes. How many square boxes match the weight of 1 rectangular box?

House MD-8
One number is a fraction bigger or smaller

In some word problems they tell you that one number is a half, or a quarter, or one-third bigger or smaller than the other number.
Here is how we write one-half: 1/2, one-third: 1/3 one-quarter, or one-fourth: 1/4
Numbers like 1/2, 1/3, 1/4 are called fractions. They are not a whole number, but pieces of a whole number.

So if you have a number, and they tell you that the other number is one half of your number, you simply divide your number by 2.

The Evil Queen has 6 poisoned apples. She gave half of her apples to the Sea Witch. How many apples did she give to the Sea Witch?
One half is 1/2. So we divide 6 apples by 2.
6 ÷ 2 = 3 The Sea Witch gets 3 apples.

Sometimes one of the numbers is one half, or one third, or one quarter bigger than the other. For example:

A witch gave her favorite bat 10 mosquitos. And that's one third of the mosquitos she gave to her favorite lizard! How many mosquitos did the witch give to the lizard?

One third is 1/3, so if 10 is one third of the other number, that means the other number is 3 times bigger than 10. 10 x 3 = 30 The witch gave 30 mosquitos to her favorite lizard.

So if number A is 1/2 of number B,
to find number A, divide B by 2
A = B ÷ 2
if A is 1/3 of B, divide B by 3
A = B ÷ 3
if A is 1/4 of B, divide B by 4
A = B ÷ 4
But if number B is 1/2 of A,
to find A, multiply B by 2
A = B x 2
if B is 1/3 of A, multiply B by 3
A = B x 3
if B is 1/4 of A, multiply B by 3
A = B x 4

Teach me multiplication! I want more!

10 x 3 I love it. Math is my favorite food!

In the following word problems, notice which number is A and which number is B:

1. *A dragonfly can eat 200 mosquitos a day, and that's only 1/3 of the mosquitos a bat can eat in one hour! How many mosquitos can a bat eat in one hour?*
So if 200 is B, and it's 1/3 of A, what do we do to find a?

2. *A lobster can live really long, but only 1/4 as long as an Ocean Quahog Clam who lives around 400 years. How long can a lobster live?*

3. *A man who is 6 feet tall is only 1/4 as tall as a giraffe. How tall is a giraffe?*

HOUSE MD-9
WE DON'T KNOW HOW MANY TIMES BIGGER OR SMALLER ONE NUMBER IS THAN THE OTHER.

They also call this kind of word problem the **Unknown Factor**.

*A magic wand costs 7 gold coins.
A spell book costs 21 gold coins.
How many times more does the spell book cost than the magic wand?*

So we are comparing two numbers, 21 and 7.
21 is a few times bigger than 7.
To find out how many times bigger,
we simply divide 21 by 7.   21 ÷ 7 = 3
So the spell book costs 3 times more
than the magic wand.

Another example:
Why is gold so expensive? Because it's rare!
*Only about 200 thousand tons of gold
have ever been mined in the whole history
of the world! Compare gold with silver:
1600 thousand tons of silver have been mined.
So how much more silver is there in the world than gold?*

We take the bigger number:
1600 thousand tons of silver,
and divide it by the smaller number -
200 thousand tons of gold.
1600 ÷ 200
Let's cross out all those zeros!
1600 ÷ 200 is the same as 16 ÷ 2 = 8
So the answer is:
There is 8 times more silver
in the world than gold!
Your turn!

1. The biggest clear cut diamond in the world is called *Cullinan 1*, or the *Great Star of Africa*. It was found in a South African mine. They measure weight of diamonds in carats, so Cullinan 1 weighs about 525 carats and it is 2.32 inches long. It is set at the top of the British royal scepter. Another amazing clear cut diamond, also one of the biggest in the world, is called *Koh-i-Noor.* It is shining on the British Royal Crown. Koh-i-Noor was found in India. It's 1.4 inches long and it weighs 105 carats.

How many times is the carat weight of Cullinan 1 bigger than the carat weight of Koh-i-Noor?

2. Dinosaurs were reptiles. They laid eggs like crocodiles or turtles. Some of their eggs didn't hatch and ended up as fossils - they turned into stone over millions of years. Archaeologists find many dinosaur eggs.

An extra large chicken egg can be 6 centimeters long. The largest dinosaur egg found is 60 centimeters long. How many times is the dinosaur egg bigger than the chicken egg?

Segnosaurus nest fossil found in England

Puzzle 4

In a square room, place 7 chairs so that there is an equal number of chairs along every wall of the room. Draw a picture!

House MD-10
two-step
multiplication and division problems

Sometimes you have to multiply twice or more to find the answer to your word problem.

There are 5 deep vaults in the castle underground. There are 4 ghosts in each vault. Each ghost screams at least 2 times during the night. How many screams do you hear every night if you happen to stay in that castle?

Let's take all the ghosts in 1 vault and see how many screams they make.
If 1 ghost makes 2 screams, 4 ghosts together make
4 x 2 = 8 screams
If all the ghosts in 1 vault make 8 screams, how many screams come from 5 vaults?
8 x 5 = 40 screams!
You won't be able to sleep all night!
So we had to multiply twice:
Ghosts in 1 vault x 2 screams each.
All the screams in 1 vault x 5 vaults.
Your turn!

1. Archaeologists found 3 secret rooms in an ancient Greek temple. In each room there was a box with 10 silver coins. The next day they found 4 more rooms. Each room had a bag of 5 gold coins. How many coins in all did the archaeologists find hidden in the temple?

2. On Halloween, a vampire showed up at a pre-school. He splashed the kids in 2 preschool classrooms with red paint. There were 15 kids in each class. They thought it was blood and screamed. Then the vampire went to the kindergarten, 1st, and 2nd grade science classes, and howled from under the teacher's desk. There were 10 kids in each class. They thought those were ghosts and ran away.
How many kids did the vampire scare in all?

If you are wondering where the preschool and the science teachers were, the Vampire chased them away pretending he was a mouse.

SQUEAK SQUEAK!

ARH-WOOO OOOOOO!

A mouse? A wolf? A science teacher?

PUZZLE 5

There are 5 apples in a basket. Divide the 5 apples between 5 kids so that each kid gets an apple, and one apple stays in the basket.

ANSWERS

AS 1
1. Forward IV steps + XII steps
4 + 12 = 16
To the right IX steps + VII steps
9 + 7 = 16

2. Forward XX steps + XV steps
20 + 15 = 35
Up the stairs III steps + XIV steps
3 + 14 = 17

AS 2
1. 14 pieces of candy
2. 9 heads
3. 27 arms

AS3
1. 3 explorers
2. 50 pet bats

AS 4
1. 41 hp
2. The missing number is 4.

AS 5
1. 11 tunnels
2. 22 white petals

AS 6
1. 5 heads
2. 12 cups of water
3. 63 Armada ships returned home to Spain

AS 7
1. The teacher was paid 21 golden rings.
It cost 1 golden ring to turn a frog into a rose.
2. 14 stars
3. Emperor Constantine bought 25 ships

AS 8
1. 5 pearls
2. 11 ships
3. 30 months

AS 9
1. 13 carrots more
2. 9 days

AS 10
1. 19 silver trees
2. the wingspan of 36 feet

AS 11
1. 10 feet
2. 8 carrots

House of Tricks 1
1. 4 minutes

House of Tricks 3
1. Turn it upside down: 999
2. The missing number is 87.
All you need to do is turn all these numbers upside down!

91 90 89 88 87 86 → THREE

3. THREE
4. The answer is 1
You are counting circles in numbers,
8 - 2 circles, 6 - 1 circle, 0 - 1 circle...
8138 - 4
6246 - 2
7027 - 1

House of Tricks 4
1. 4 cats
2. Very large hands.

House of Tricks 5
1. Trip 1: The two boys cross to the other side of the river.
Boy 1 stays on the other side.
Trip 2: Boy 2 brings the boat back to this side of the river.
On this side, the boy gets out of the boat, and one soldier
gets into the boat.
Trip 3: The soldier crosses to the other side.
Over there, the soldier gets out of the boat,
and Boy 1 gets into the boat.
Trip 4: Boy 1 brings the boat back to this side of the river,
picks up Boy 2, and
Trip 5: Boy 1 and Boy 2 go together to the other side
of the river. Boy 1 stays there.
Trip 6: Boy 2 brings the boat to this side of the river again.
He gets out, and the next soldier gets into the boat
to go to the other side.
And they repeat this until all soldiers cross the river.

House of Tricks 6
1. 3 minutes: If every minute the quantity
of the potion doubles, at 3 minutes we have
half the cauldron, and at 4 minutes the full cauldron.

MD 1
1. $1 = 2000 cowry shells
2. 8000 seeds

MD 2
1. 5 columns of poisoned apples
2. 4-leaf lucky clovers

MD 3
1. 10 bags of scorpions
2. 8 apples

MD 4
1. 8 hands
2. 25 miles per hour

MD 5
1. 5 pirates
2. 4 mushrooms

MD 6
1. 15 wolves
2. 60 baby mice

MD 7
1. Mariana Trench is 35 thousand feet deep, and in some places 36 thousand and even more!
2. Brachiosaurus was 80 feet long.

MD 8
1. 600 mosquitos
2. 100 years

MD 9
1. more than 5 times
2 10 times

MD 10
1. 50 coins
2. 60 kids

Puzzle 1
When the barrel is exactly half-full, the surface
of water divides the barrel into two equal parts.
So if you tilt the barrel in a way that the surface of water
connects the bottom point of the barrel rim
and the top point of its bottom, the water surface
divides the barrel into two equal half, and the barrel
is half-full.
A. half-full B. not enough water C. too much water

 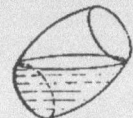 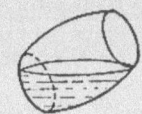 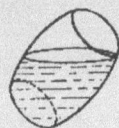

Puzzle 2

If all bicycles on the playground had 2 wheels,
there would be 8 x 2 = 16 wheels on the playground.
But we have 21 wheels.
How many extra wheels do we have? 21 - 16 = 5
Guess what: those extra wheels
are the wheels from tricycles!
So now we know there were 5 tricycles.
And how many bicycles?
8 - 5 = 3
So there were 5 tricycles and 3 bicycles on the playground.

Puzzle 3

Puzzle 4

If one of the chairs stands in the corner, there are 2 chairs by each wall! Tricked you!

Puzzle 5
One of the kids will get an apple together with the basket, this way 1 apple will remain in the basket!

Thank you for reading this book!

www.ingramcontent.com/pod-product-compliance
Lightning Source LLC
Chambersburg PA
CBHW041504010526

44118CB00001B/18